The Rhythm Of Two Heartbeats

Unspoken Words Of Sweet Sixteen

ELZA MARY JOSEPH

/ BookLeaf
Publishing

India | USA | UK

Made with ❤ on the BookLeaf Publishing Platform
www.bookleafpub.in
www.bookleafpub.com

Dedication

To my family, friends and well wishers - this book is for you, with all my heart.

Preface

This book was born from the various seasons of my life, where I faced *love* and *loss*, *beginnings* and *endings*. Each poem carries a fragment of me, a memory, a scar and a moment, I wish to preserve in words.

Writing poems became my way of coping in this world. Some poems speak about my family and friends who stood by me, when no one else did. Some speak of friendships which slipped away, which stayed only to teach me something. Some speak of memories too bitter to be true. Together, they create a beautiful rhythm, *a rhythm of two heartbeats*, connections and separations, which I hold close to my heart.

I hope you find a glimpse of yourselves in each word that I have written. I hope they serve as a reminder that everything has its own time, and that no pain is permanent.

May these poems be a shoulder for you to cry on, to hold your hand in silence and to bring you hope.

Acknowledgements

To my dad, for his quite strength, for teaching me resilience and allowing me to find my own path. Your lessons and words echo throughout this book.

To my mom, for her endless love. Your unwavering faith in me and your words of comfort has not only shaped who I am, but how I see the world. Your love and hugs live in these pages.

Achu, thank you for the laughter that brightened my dim days, for being my quite support. Thank *you* for showing me that family is forever no matter the distance and time. Your presence in my life is a gift I carry close to my heart.

To my friends, *the past and the present,* thank you for the laughter, the lessons and the moments that have shaped my heart.

Finally, to every *reader* who lifts up this book. May you find a piece of yourselves in this book, may they remind you that even in the darkest seasons, hope and love endure.

Sculpted

I am a girl sculpted from clay
So beautifully crafted by God himself
With every little pressure
He made sure I am perfect
With every little curve
He made sure I am loved

I am a girl sculpted from clay
So beautifully crafted by God himself
With a bit of sparkle
He made sure I would glow
With a bit of magic
He made sure I would stand out

I am a girl sculpted from clay
So beautifully crafted by God himself
With a gift of light
He made sure I had a heart to hold
With a man's missing rib
He made sure I was known

Almost Fifteen

Fifteen felt so far away
Now in a week, it's my birthday
Don't know what to feel
It still feels unreal
Still a little girl
Who gets excited when she finds a pearl
Hold onto my mom's hand
When I walk through the sand
And lay on my dad's chest
Feeling so blessed
Hugging my brother so tight
Don't want this to end by tonight

Plushie

Sitting on her bed,
I see her every day,
With a silent dream
Of hoping someday
Someone will hold her
Through her sorrow and fragility,
A gentle hand in her silent vulnerability.

I see her sadness, her laughter, her tears.
I see her hopes, her fears.
I watch her work tirelessly,
Dream endlessly,
Yet carry the weight quietly.

If only I could speak,
I would let the world know
Of the storms she braves,
The battles she hides,
The pain she endures
That no one else seems to realize.

Stitches

I entered the room I feared I would
All I saw were endless items
Whispering my name

As I picked each one,
They revealed their hidden beauty
The leather bag, my brother gave
The little camel, dad brought home
The house I once shared with my mom

And in the corner, there stood a teddy bear
Do you remember that?
The one you gave me,
When you promised to stay,
To never break my heart

The teddy bear, that flushed my head
With the memories of our past
Each stitch reminded me of the love
We couldn't hold onto.

Departure

I think we let people go,
Not because they're not what you dreamt of
But because it's easier

It's easier to leave than to fight
It's easier to leave than to take responsibility
It's easier to leave than to take accountability
It's easier to leave than to prove yourself
It's easier to leave than to face the harsh truth

It's easier to leave than to face uncertainty
It's easier to leave than to stay
It's easier to fold our hearts and simply walk away

Hold

It's not because he felt like home
It's not because he said goodbye first
It's not because he loved you first
It's not because he fell harder
It's not because the universe made you feel guilty
It's not because we grew apart
It's all because I held on too tightly when you were
already letting go.

This book is for the ones who sit in the rain, trying to understand other people's pain. For those who sometimes wish to disappear, but find themselves crying instead. For the ones who care too much about unfinished stories and drown in the memories that once made them happy. It's for the hearts that hope—quietly, desperately—that one day, someone will see them as a person, not as a set of assumptions in someone else's eyes.

Echoes

Deep inside a quiet heart,
Lies the echoes of a childhood start.

With an aching pain that won't subside,
I wonder when the feelings died.

Moments burning like a bright flame,
Not feeling just the same.

I hold on to the rest of me,
Cause that's all there will ever be.

The feeling of wanting to stay,
But it'll never be the same as that day.

Veil

Behind the mask of a woman
Is a small little girl
Wondering when her childhood ended
When the duties of a queen
Landed on her back
Giving her the aching pain
Still, she whispers to herself
"I am here."
In the shadows where dreams linger,
She weaves a tapestry of grace,
Hiding the tears of yesterday,
Embracing strength in every trace.
Through the tempest, she strides anew,
Carving paths with fragile hands,
For beneath the crown's heavy weight,
Her spirit quietly understands.

Goodbye

It feels so broken
And my words are unspoken
I feel the need to be apart
Just to learn the rhythm of my heart

I start my day with a cry
Staring into the very blue sky
Hoping the feelings would end
Although, time may never mend

All I want is to be free
Like the waves kiss the sea
I know I'll have to say goodbye
Even if I don't know why

Horizon

The sun is bright, and the sky is clear
With a gentle breeze I hold dear

The flowers will bloom in mere days
Sunlight dancing with gentle rays
The feeling of joy is found in small things
Like the blooming flowers and when the birds all sing

Life is good, with no need to hide
Every memory sparkles far and wide

Always Home

Beneath the whispers of the night,
I hold you close to my heart, so sweet
Memories wander and lie,
When the sky whispers your name
A sound both familiar and comforting

I remember the dinners we spent together
And how we all cramped up in one bed
These memories still linger, as if time never passed
Filling my heart with endless joy
A gentle reminder that no matter the distance nor time
My family is always home to me.

Bond

Through laughter and teary days
You made me smile in countless ways
When storms had risen and skies turned gray
Your faith and love never faded away

We share our goals, both big and small
Never letting each other fall
Though secrets echo through the jokes we'd send
I found my heart within a friend

For in this life, where roads may be curved and bent
I'm blessed to walk it till the end
With my family's care that'll never end

When the years keep moving through,
I shall cherish every laugh with you

Everlasting

I thought we would never part,
But now we did, and it broke my heart

I miss the days we used to stay over
We stayed up late, just you and me
The talks, the laughs, and the endless dreams
Longing for a world, we hoped we'd see

Although we were never meant to stay,
Your light still guides me every day.

A friend like you is hard to find
But memories still live in my heart and mind.

Hollow

I hear your voice in the quiet rain
A reminder wrapped in pain
Your face still lingers, faint but clear
A ghost of joy, I hold with a tear

The nights seem long, yet the stars don't gleam
Still, I see you in every dream
I try to reach you, and the air turns cold
A bitter memory left untold

Now silence stays where love had been,
An empty ache beneath my skin.

Miles

You've flown afar to chase your dream,
But home feels empty, or so it seems.
I wait for calls, for jokes we share,
Wishing you were simply here.

I hope you find your way back to us
Through every storm, I keep my trust
Life's not the same, and thus I see
No one could take your place with me.

Faded Rivers

We carved our names on bark and stones
Swore we'd never walk and be alone
But weathers change, seasons shift and hearts can stray
Even rivers sometimes lose their way

We wandered the fields that the sun had kissed
Our laughter wrapped in twilight's mist
The world seemed young, our hearts were too
The sky was wide so dreams we drew

Now I pass the trails we knew
The stars still burn, but just not for you

Forever

I reminisce the memories I shared with you under the
sun
The moments we've shared and just endless fun

Even though you're still there
You've wandered far from here

Distance may keep us apart
But you still live in my heart

Afterglow

I walk through the streets we used to know,
The laughter still echoes, but the shadows grow

I wonder what this time may mean
Between the memories and the sights unseen

I hope I find it in me, not to hate
To hold the past softly and to not tempt fate

It's feels like I've been holding on for far too long
But my mind stills reminisces that one song

Too bittersweet to not let go
Holding pieces of a past I know.

The skies have started to bid goodbye, a gentle way to let the feelings dry. Every ending folds into a start, a chance to mend, to heal the heart. Steps untraveled lie wide and clear, each one a promise, each one sincere. The past may linger, but it won't bind, for new horizons await the mind. With open eyes, face the day, and let the sunrise guide you—start this chapter fresh, with hope, courage, and a heart ready to embrace what comes next.

Eighth

Eight hearts I held, eight stories told,
The eighth one slipped; I let them go.
I wore the fault, I bear the pain,
Each memory burns like summer rain.
I speak their name in silent rooms,
Haunted by the echo of faded blooms.
Yet even in this weight I bear,
A seed of change is planted there.
Though I lost friends, and I know it's true,
I'll rise again—though scarred, renewed.

Haven

I always say too little and smiled too wide,
I let truth and fear both coincide.
Though the distance wouldn't stay,
Yet some goodbyes just fade away.

You stood there waiting, with eyes true and kind,
While pride and worry crossed my mind.
I meant to speak, I wanted to make things right,
But as the clock struck twelve, I let it fade into the night.

The weeks have passed, the words still near,
The ache once sharp is now unclear.
I still remember, yes, a bit,
But even that sting begins to sit.

Time shows me how to let things be,
The past is past, it comforts me.
A gentle smile replaces pain,
And what we had, I still retain.

Ron

Tiny paws that danced on floors,
Warm snuggles pressed against closed doors.

A curly tail, a snort, a grin,
The little heart that beat within.

Your eyes would shine with endless glee,
A world of love reflected in thee.

Through walks and naps, through sunlit days,
You filled my life in countless ways.

Though now your bark is soft and still,
Your memory lingers, warm and real.

I hear your paws in quiet dreams,
Your spirit near in moonlit beams.

Forever loved, forever missed,
A little soul I can't resist.

Goodbye for now, but not the end,
You'll always be my little friend.

Sunrise

Golden rays spill through the trees,
A gentle hum drifts on the breeze.
Birds awake with cheerful song,
The world feels right, the day feels long.
Flowers stretch in colors bright,
Dewdrops sparkle in the light.
Laughter drifts from streets below,
Hearts are warm, the spirits glow.
Every moment feels brand new,
A sky of pink, a cloud of blue.
Life unfolds with simple cheer,
A sunlit morning, full and clear.

Charlie

I hear your chirp in quiet hours,
Soft and bright like morning flowers.
Though wings have carried you afar,
Your spirit hums where memories are.
I close my eyes, I feel you near,
A little warmth, a whisper clear.
Charlie, my friend, my tiny light,
You shine for me in the silent night.

Alone

Alone in the corner of my room,
I let the quiet settle around me.

The world goes on, unaware,
While my tears trace paths down my cheeks,
Soft and warm.

Each drop carries a memory,
A longing, a hurt I cannot speak.

The silence is heavy,
Yet somehow comforting,
Holding me like a fragile friend.

I breathe in the emptiness,
Release the ache into the shadows,
And for a moment,
I am just here,
Just feeling,
Just letting it be.

Chaos and Quiet

The city roars outside my window,
Horns blaring, engines rumbling,
But inside, the room smells of old paper and rain,
And the hum of memories swirls in the air.

I touch the velvet of a forgotten scarf,
Soft against my fingers,
And taste the bitterness of coffee,
That lingers like unanswered questions.

Laughter and shouting drift from the street,
But my chest tightens with a different sound ,
The hollow echo of longing,
The quiet pulse of something lost.

Sunlight fractures through the glass,
Sharp and warm and blinding all at once,
And I wonder if chaos and calm,
Are two sides of the same coin,
Flipping endlessly in my hands.

Once you've felt the weight of a feeling, you can sense it before it arrives. Once you've known abandonment, you recognize its shadow long before it appears. The cruel part is that no one truly understands, no matter how much they try. You warn them you'll be left behind, and they keep insisting, "I'll never go." But am I really so easy to forget? Did I ever matter so little? Maybe it's safer to keep my heart closed, to let no one inside.

Sorry

It's a word, maybe an apology,
Maybe a heartfelt regret,
About the things which took place.

It may mend the strong surface,
But we don't show the cracks underneath, do we?

A sorry, can make things look okay,
But it's still not quiet the same.

We patch them up with silence,
And smile like everything's fine.

And maybe that's what growing is ,
To learn that healing hurts.

That peace can bloom from broken soil,
But never without the dirt.

So keep your sorry, I've heard it all,

And maybe I'll whisper mine too.

Not to undo what's been done,
Just to remember what was true.

And maybe that's what growing is,
To learn that healing hurts.

That peace can bloom from broken soil,
But never without the dirt.

Half-Drawn

A singer's almost is an unfinished song.
A painter's almost is an incomplete painting.
An author's almost is an unfinished book.

We were a masterpiece left half-drawn,
A melody that paused mid-song.
Every word we meant to say,
Still hums between the night and day.

Maybe "almost" is its own kind of art,
Where beauty hides inside the lack.
Where love is not a perfect start,
But knowing we can't have it back.

So let the song stay half-complete,
Let the canvas show what might have been.
Because even the pause, the ache, the heat,
Are proof that we have been.

Tomorrow

Tomorrow might be cruel, or hard, or worse,
And every night before I close my eyes,
I whisper a prayer into the dark,
Not for answers, just for peace disguised.

I ask, will you be gentle, please?
Will you spare me from the weight I dread?
Will you keep the ache from growing deep,
And hush the storms inside my head?

Sometimes, I fear your heavy hands,
How you tear the hours I build apart.
You come too fast, without my will,
And press your cold against my heart.

I pray that when you take my name,
You'll speak it soft, not as a curse.
That when I wake within your arms,
You'll teach me that it could be worse.

Ink

I write when my mouth can't express,
what my heart wants to.

I write when I have a feeling so deep,
that don't know what to do anymore.

I write when my eyes speak,
all the emotions that my mouth couldn't.

I write when my eyes carry the weight,
my back can't anymore.

I write when I feel lonely,
when no one had any idea what was going on.

I write when my bag is too heavy to hold,
and I can't bear the weight anymore.

Everywhere

Five homes, four schools,
Fifteen years stitched across walls I barely remember.
My life is scattered like leaves in the wind,
Everywhere, nowhere, and in-between.

I've carried suitcases heavier than my own shoulders,
Moved through hallways with faces that fade,
Friendships that bloomed like brief sparks
And vanished before I could hold them.

Each home promised comfort,
But I only unpacked pieces of myself,
Leaving the rest behind
In rooms that were never mine to keep.

Sometimes I dream of a place
Where doors don't change,
Where hands reach for me and stay,
And where "home" isn't just a word
I whisper to myself at night.

But until then, I wander—
A collector of fleeting memories,
A stranger in familiar places,
Searching for a belonging I've yet to find.

At First

When I first saw you, I didn't notice the quiet storms
that lived behind your eyes,
I didn't see the depth of love you carried quietly for the
world,
I didn't see the ache and pain that shaped every careful
word you spoke,
I didn't see what your heart longed for, or the dreams
you held close and feared to share.

I didn't care at the time, because all I could feel,
Were endless poems rushing toward me like rivers of
light,
Words and emotions tumbling forward, begging to be
understood,
To offer me a chance I hadn't known I needed.

A chance to learn the true meaning of love,
A chance to understand the weight of someone else's
hurt,
A chance to confront my own broken pieces and mend

them slowly,
To become a better, kinder version of myself, someone
worthy of you.

Remain

I don't love you the way you deserved to be loved,
I don't love you the way you love me,
I don't love you the way I love my friends.

Because you're my family — my forever.
You're the people who have carried every version of me,
The ones who've seen my laughter, my silence, my
breaking.

You've been there through the shifts of seasons,
Through the fading of faces I once called my friends.

From the beginning, till the very end,
You've stayed, not out of duty, but out of love,
Out of something that doesn't need words or promises,
Something deeper, quieter, more real.

After broken friendships and a shattered heart,
After nights spent wishing for belonging,
I find it here — in you.

Because when everything else leaves,
You're the ones who remain.

Go

I've carried enough of your shadows,
Listened enough to your storms.

It's time to step out of my quiet,
To leave the space I've claimed for myself.

Go, and let both our hearts breathe free.

Healing

The joy of childhood stretches wide,
Running barefoot through endless fields,
Laughing loud and free beneath the sun,
Chasing butterflies and the wind alike,
Finding small wonders in the simplest, ordinary
moments,
A hidden magic in the corners of a day.
It's hard to thread a path between
The weight of past pain and the lightness of innocent
happiness,
Yet each moment of wonder feels like quiet healing,
A gentle therapy for a tired heart,
A reminder that even after sorrow,
The world still holds laughter, warmth, and play.

I'm deeply grateful that you've reached the middle of
this book. It means more than words can capture,
because every page was written with a piece of my heart,
a part of my thoughts, and a hope that they might touch
someone. I hope, in some small way, these words have
reached you—resonated, comforted, or even simply made
you pause and reflect. Just knowing that this journey has
brought us to the same point fills me with gratitude, and
I hope that whatever you've taken from these pages
carries a little light into your own story.

Rekindle

It didn't happen all at once, not like the stories told, there weren't any sudden movement of light, breaking in through the dark.

It was way quieter than that, like the way we accidently laugh out loud in the middle of a long conversation with some friends.

Like remembering the lyrics of a song, I once used to love, and realizing the ache in every word isn't there anymore.

Yet, there are still days, when the weight of everything, falls right back on your shoulders, without any warning whatsoever. And I find myself fall back into quiet, wondering if I've really moved forward at all.

Healing doesn't rush, it lingers.
It builds up slowly, through the cracks of pain, you swore you would never close.

It comes in moments, too small to notice, until one day,
you're laughing loud again, and you don't stop yourself
this time.

And maybe that's all healing ever is.
Not the return of who you were,
But the gentle discovery of who you're still becoming.
Piece by piece, smile by smile,
Learning to live again, in the quiet beauty of it all.

Quiet

You didn't slam the door, nor did you scream.
You left quietly, you closed the door slowly, and just left.
Your absence became louder than any goodbye.

The text left on 'read' still haunts me to this day.
I replay our last moments in my head,
Searching for something I could have said,
Something that might have made you stay.

But the quiet between us grew heavier with each
passing hour,
And your absence filled every space you once held.

I catch glimpses of you in ordinary places,
And for a second, it feels like you never left,
Before the emptiness settles back in.

Silence

Silence isn't empty.
It is the weight of all the words we never said,
The echo of laughter that faded before it reached
anyone,
The pause between heartbeats where everything lingers,
And we feel it even when we don't understand it.

It drapes over rooms like a heavy cloth,
Filling corners, settling in the cracks,
Curling around chairs, around doors,
Around the spaces we thought were ours alone.

It remembers who we were,
Who we tried to be,
Who we hid from,
Even when no one else did.

Losing someone leaves a silence that words can't fill, a space in your days that no one else can occupy. It's not just the absence of their presence, but the echo of everything you once shared—the laughter, the arguments, the small, ordinary moments that now feel impossibly distant. Memories can sting as much as they comfort, and sometimes it feels like moving forward is a betrayal, while staying still feels unbearable. Yet, in that ache, there's also a strange tenderness: a reminder of how deeply you loved, how fully you allowed them into your life, and how their mark on you will remain, quietly shaping the person you continue to become.

Me

Some mornings I still wake heavy, feeling smaller than the world, but then sunlight spills through the window and I remember I'm still here, still breathing, still trying.

I catch myself laughing at nothing, or crying over everything, and I realize life and grief can sit together without one swallowing the other.

The small things start to matter again—the smell of rain, a song I love, the way my own heartbeat reminds me I'm alive—and I feel pieces of me returning, quiet, stubborn, alive.

I'm not the same as before, I carry the hollows grief left behind, but I carry windows too, letting in light I thought I'd lost forever, and slowly, I am learning to be me again.

Pieces

I carry myself in pieces, in laughter, in joy, in pain.

In memories that linger like quiet ghosts,

In habits that remind me I am still here even when I forget,

In moments I didn't think I would survive but somehow did.

I am contradictions walking, sorrow brushing against hope,

Soft joy hiding where no one notices, ache humming quietly through my chest,

And still, I am learning that carrying all of it, all the pieces of me,

Is not weakness but proof that I am alive, that I am here,

That I am enough, even when I feel broken.

Companion

Time walks beside me quietly, never shouting, never
pushing,
its steps measured, patient, brushing against mine like a
gentle reminder
that moments stretch and shrink, that yesterday still
hums in the air,
and tomorrow waits just beyond the corner, silent but
present.
I feel it in the rhythm of my breath, in the pulse of the
city streets,
in the shadow of a tree that remembers summers I
barely held,
in the way a song suddenly brings me back to a room
I've long forgotten,
and I realize that even in absence, even in loss, time
carries me,
its presence soft, persistent, like a hand brushing against
my shoulder
telling me I am here, I am moving, I am still becoming.

The Open Window

There, a window stood open,
and only one thought popped into my head.

I couldn't do it anymore.
Nobody needs me, not even my partner.

Life would move on,
even if I wasn't there.

I don't have to endure this pain,
I don't have to face challenges ,
I have a choice.

I can either stay and be miserable, or
I can leave and be happy, forever.

There a window stood open,
all I had to do was jump.

Undone

How do you explain,
that feeling of pain?

When you were left with a choice,
of noise and joys.

But you didn't know what to choose,
you had to look for a clue.

It wasn't there though,
you had to take it slow.

The joys couldn't be forgotten,
but it's forbidden.

You were certain,
it hurt you more than the person.

When life pushed you down,
you wore the pain like a crown.

You held on though it stung,
carrying battles unsung,
yet a part of you stayed undone.

Unforgiven

Do you remember
The night we talked together
The night I thought was unforgettable
It turned into a nightmare
Something I prayed would never happen

I lost you in the midst of my heartbeat
The one who once made me happy
Is now a ghost that lives rent free in my mind

Oh darling, I hate myself
I hate myself for leaving you, for making it true
I hate myself for lying to your face
I hate myself because I never had faith in us
I hate myself because all I ever did was wrong

It hurts to live life without you, by my side
I know I made you leave
I know you hate me now
I hate that I hold on to hope at the last moment

Linger

It hurts
The silence between prayers and promises
The distance between you and me
The aching pain in my heart
The silent talks between our hearts
The promises I made are still wandering
Waiting for my prayers to find it
The prayers have travelled miles and miles
Yet couldn't find the faded ones
With every breath, I smell yourself
With every touch, I remember yours
With every smile, I wonder yours
With every tear, I miss you more

I walk alone,
yet feel your trace,
a quiet echo
I can't erase.

Unsaid

It wasn't the day you left,
It wasn't the day she told you to do it,
It wasn't even the silence that followed your name.

It was the grief that came with it.

While I was caught up in processing it,
Your friends made sure it was hard for me.

Every stare, every whisper
They all just made me feel alone.

Maybe they only brushed against my body,
But it hurt within too.

Shadow

There's a shadow that follows me,
Everyday, everywhere.

It's always there, like a little friend,
But one, I always seem to dread.

It's made of yesterdays I can't erase,
And memories too bitter.

All seems fine,
But I'm breaking inside.

I wish to show you,
What I hold within.

Distance

I held it in for too long,
The unsaid words. the silent goodbyes,
The secrets I hold within, the friendships lost,
The distance between you and me.

You knew it too,
Yet did the exact same,
The hands that once held me, are out of reach,
The voice once familiar, has now become a memory to
remember.

Unsent

I wrote you letters I never sent
Each page, heavy with words.
Whenever I pick them up,
They tremble in my hand.

Just the sight of your name,
Gives me a whole lot to reminisce.
The eyes that spoke, and small talks.
Every tear that screamed your name.

Forgive

I kept the apology you never gave,
Not because I regretted leaving you,
But because I wanted closure.
To put an end to our "almost"
Which never came around, to be honest.

What if forgiving means forgetting too?
What if, in order to forgive you,
I have to forget even the sound of your name?

Your name carries weight.
The kind of weight I want to bear.
Forgetting you would mean forgetting a part of me.

Unfamiliar

The door still opens the same,
But it doesn't know my hands anymore.
The walls hum with laughter that isn't mine,
And every step I take echoes like a memory out of place.

I try to breathe in comfort,
But all I find is dust and distance,
And I realise — maybe homes don't change,
Maybe I just grew out of the person who belonged here.

Cherished

A person I once called mine,
A name I once adored,
A presence that taught me who I am,
A laugh that still echoes softly,
A glance that lingers in corners of memory,
A warmth that comes back in quiet moments,
A memory I hold close to my heart.

Unbound

She moves quietly through the rooms,
feet barely touching the floor,
eyes trained not to meet the sharpness
of voices that cut deeper than knives,
hands always folded, shoulders hunched,
a body trained in silence,
a soul rehearsing apologies for things she didn't do.

The walls remember everything —
the slammed doors, the whispered threats,
the trembling laughter she forced herself to give,
the nights spent counting ceiling cracks
because sleep was too dangerous,
and dreams were luxuries she wasn't allowed.

She forgets what her voice sounds like,
her own name almost foreign on her lips,
her thoughts trimmed and tamed
to fit inside the narrow cage of fear
built by the person who promised love

but delivered control,
and the years slip past like sand through fingers
that never touched the sun.

But one morning, something shifts —
a memory, a song, a smile glimpsed in a stranger,
a whisper from herself saying,
"Your life was never meant for these walls,
your wings were never meant to fold."

She sees the door not as a barrier,
but as an invitation,
the hallway stretching into possibility,
the windows wide, letting in air she thought she lost,
and for the first time, trembling becomes strength,
fear becomes fuel,
and she steps forward, each footfall a promise
to herself,
to the life she was always allowed to take.

The walls no longer cage her,
they stand behind her, witness to a story rewritten,
a body unburdened, a voice reclaiming space,
and in the quiet after,
she realizes she is more than the sum of broken rooms,
more than the echoes of shouted commands,
more than the fear she carried like a second skin.

She walks into sunlight that tastes like freedom,
air that feels like possibility,
and the world, wide and waiting,
reminds her that even after years of being told
otherwise,
she can finally choose herself.

Chosen

Don't expect me to be perfect,
I will stumble, I will fall and I will have quiet tantrums
within me,
Just please, promise me that you will hold space for it
and not try to fix me.

Don't try to change the way I love,
Or the way my thoughts wander at night,
Because that's what makes me whole.

Don't forget that I'm not yours to own,
Just a partner who'll walk beside you,
Through everything.

I need you to do the same for me,
Walk beside me, not in front, not behind,
With me, equally

Do, however, see me,
Really see me, in laughter, in silence, in everything I

don't say,
And love the parts of me i hide from the world,
Because i will give you my heart,
Not because i am perfect,
But because you choose to stay anyway.

Still

I leave these pages here, scattered pieces of myself,
words that trembled in silence, words that screamed
softly into the dark,
laughter that found its way through tears,
memories that bruised and healed me in equal measure,
and all the moments I thought I would forget
now sit folded between the lines,
reminders that even broken pieces carry light.

I walked through rooms that didn't recognize me,
through nights that taught me how to hold my own
heartbeat,
through storms that whispered I wasn't enough,
and yet here I am, still breathing, still holding
the fragile pulse of everything I've learned,
everything I've lost, everything I've loved.

I hope these words reach you in some small way,
even if you never read them,
even if they never touch another soul,

they exist as proof that I survived,
that I felt, that I grew,
that I am still mine —
a life larger than fear,
larger than pain,
larger than the walls that tried to keep me quiet.

And as the book closes,
I exhale, quietly, fully,
and carry myself forward,
into sunlight I didn't know I deserved,
into a world that waits for the pieces of me
to find their home,
and I smile, softly,
because even endings are beginnings,
and I am still here,
still breathing, still becoming,
still free.

Anew

I saw windows everywhere,
But I never took it as a sign.
Until recently, something shifted in me,
I began to find the hidden beauty in things.

The window was not just glass or frame
It was a chance, a door, an invitation,
A new opportunity for me to rise,
To stretch my wings and finally fly.

Whispers

There's a difference,
Between thoughts and words,
Between saying and holding back.

Unspoken words feel both safe and painful,
Like whispers trapped inside your chest,
Never fully escaping,
Yet shaping every quiet moment.

Amidst the gentle breeze,
You are reminded of what you never said,
Of all the subtle moments
When you quietly longed for closure,
And all you hold are memories—
Endless, lingering, tender memories.

Take a moment, breathe.

These pages hold fragments of my heart, but they may
also mirror yours.

In them, you may see your own pain, your quiet sorrows,
the moments you felt lost or unseen.

You may feel the joy that comes in small, fleeting ways,
the love that shaped you, the losses that still echo.

Remember that it is okay to feel everything at once, to
hold both grief and hope, fear and courage.

These words are here not to fix you, but to remind you
that your feelings are real, valid, and shared,
that in every shadow, there is a spark waiting for you to
notice, and in every ending, a beginning quietly waits.

Translucent

I've learned to smile through the cracks,
To hold my breath when the world gets loud,
To pretend that breaking is just another form of
breathing.

People see me and say, "you're strong,"
But they don't see the way my hands shake
When the silence becomes too heavy to hold.

I've been fragile for years,
Glass skin and trembling bones,
Trying to hold the weight of too many goodbyes.

They said pain makes you beautiful,
But I think it just makes you quieter.

Testament

Every poem I write is a piece of me,
A whisper I couldn't say aloud,
A bruise I hid beneath metaphors,
A memory that still lingers in the lines.

They think it's just ink on paper,
But it's every night I cried quietly,
Every smile that didn't quite reach my eyes,
Every heartbeat that tried to make sense of love and
loss.

My poems speak my story,
In ways I never could.
They hold the versions of me I outgrew,
And the ones I'm still learning to forgive.

Sometimes I read them back and see ghosts,
Sometimes I see healing.
Either way, they are all me,

The girl who kept feeling,
Even when the world told her not to.

Found Family

They aren't bound to me by blood,
But by laughter that fills the cracks in my heart,
By the way they stay when the world feels too loud,
By the quiet comfort of knowing I'm understood.

We've shared broken pieces and called it healing,
Shared late-night talks that felt like prayer,
Held each other's pain without asking for reasons,
Because sometimes love needs no explanation.

Anchor

He is the quiet in my chaos,
The shoulder I didn't know I needed,
The laughter that breaks through the storm.

Even when words fail,
He understands the spaces between my thoughts,
The weight I carry without saying a thing.

He teases, he pushes, he protects,
And sometimes I forget to say it,
How much it means to have him.

Not just as a brother,
But as a steady hand,
A reminder that no matter how far I wander,
Someone here knows me,
And waits.

Home

She is the spark in ordinary days,
The laughter that lingers long after the joke is gone,
The hand that reaches for mine
When the world feels too heavy to hold alone.

With her, silence isn't empty,
It's comfortable, full of understanding
That words aren't always necessary
When someone truly sees you.

She knows my cracks, my chaos, my quiet fears,
And still chooses to stay,
To walk beside me through storms,
To celebrate the small victories,
To remind me of joy when I almost forget it.

She is more than friendship,
She is home in human form,
A heart that chose me
Even when I was too messy to deserve it.

Stayed

Not everyone did,
But to the ones who did,
Thank you for being there, with me.

Through silences,
Through my half answered texts,
Through the calls I cut in between.

They stayed,
Not demanding, not loudly,
But in the quiet ways that mattered most,
The "take care" after a long day,
The random hugs once or twice,

And I've learned
It's not the people who say they'll never leave,
But the ones who stay even when you do,
Who show you what love really looks like.

Because staying isn't about forever,

It's about choosing you again and again,
Even when it's hard to.

Versions

I'm not who I was,
The friendships I've been through,
The lessons I've learnt,
And the quite moments that have shaped my heart,
Have changed who I am and who I'll become.

I carry the echoes of every goodbye,
The warmth of every laugh,
And the silence of things left unsaid.

I've outgrown versions of myself
That once fit too tightly,
Learned that not all endings are tragedies,
Some are quiet beginnings in disguise.

And though I'm still learning to forgive the past,
I know now that change isn't loss,
It's becoming.

Seasons

Some people aren't meant to stay,
but that doesn't mean it wasn't real.
It just means some people are chapters,
and not the book.

There are people who pass through you quietly,
like seasons that forget to say goodbye.
To build something beautiful,
even if it wasn't built to last.

Untamed

The flowers in the wild never wait for applause,
they bloom because they were always meant to.
No stranger's hand, no gentle praise,
just sunlight, rain, and their own quiet will to live.

I think about that sometimes,
how they rise from cracked earth,
unnoticed, unseen, yet still radiant,
as if beauty doesn't need witnesses to exist.

Maybe we're meant to be like that too—
to grow without permission,
to find our own light when the world forgets to offer
any,
to bloom not because someone asked us to,
but because we can.

Perhaps strength isn't loud,
perhaps it's the quiet courage of a wildflower,
that keeps growing in a place,

where nothing else thought it could.

And maybe that's what it means to live,
to bloom anyway,
even when no one is watching.

To Everything

I carry pieces of everyone I've known,
woven quietly into the edges of my heart,
threads of laughter, echoes of heartbreak,
moments that have shaped me,
even when I didn't realize I was changing.

My family, the ones who loved me,
even when I was too stubborn to be loved,
who held me without needing words,
who stayed even when I walked away,
you are the soil I grew from,
the roots that remind me where I belong.

And my friends—the chosen ones,
the laughter that fills up quiet rooms,
the hands that reached for me,
when I had nothing left to give myself,
the ones who saw the messy, unpolished me,
and decided, anyway, to stay.
You have been my refuge, my storm, my anchor,

proof that love doesn't need a reason,
to exist, just a heart willing to hold it.

To those who left,
I carry you softly too,
not with anger, not with regret,
but with gratitude I only understand now.
You were lessons wrapped in human form,
reminders that not all people are meant to stay,
that loss can be gentle,
that endings are sometimes beginnings in disguise.

And to the ones who stayed,
you are the quiet miracle,
the heartbeat that reminded me to keep going,
when the world felt like too much.
Your patience, your laughter, your unshakable presence
taught me that love can be steady,
even when life is messy.

To the moments between,
the heartbreak and the joy,
the sunsets I watched alone,
the songs that carried my tears,
the nights of endless thought,
and mornings of gentle hope,
you have made me brave,

in ways I never saw coming.

So here I am, holding all of you,
the people, the lessons, the love, the losses,
wrapped into the person I am becoming,
grateful for every shadow and every light,
every step I took, every hand I held,
every heart that touched mine,
and taught me what it means to be alive.

Cheers to everything,
to the laughter, the pain, the quiet, the chaos,
to the people who came, the people who stayed,
to the ones I lost and the ones I found,
to all of it,
because without all of it,
I wouldn't be me.